UNLOCK THE ANIMAL WORLD

"All around us, all the time, animals are embarking on remarkable journeys, having important conversations, forming lasting friendships, showing love to their families, working hard, and having fun. How wonderful it is to get a small glimpse into their lives. And how important it is to let them live in peace."

INGRID NEWKIRK

UNLOCK THE ANIMAL WORLD

Incredible Facts for Young Superheroes

INGRID NEWKIRK

First published in India by HarperCollins *Publishers* 2026
HarperCollins Publishers India, Cyber City,
Building 10-A, Gurugram, Haryana – 122002, India

www.harpercollins.co.in

2 4 6 8 10 9 7 5 3 1

P-ISBN: 978-93-7307-450-4
E-ISBN: 978-93-7307-133-6

Typeset in 11/14 Adobe Caslon Pro at
HarperCollins *Publishers* India

Printed and bound at
Saurabh Printers Pvt. Ltd.

This book is produced from independently certified FSC® paper to ensure responsible forest management.
HarperCollins Publishers, Macken House, 39/40 Mayor Street Upper, Dublin 1, D01 C9W8, Ireland

Table of Contents

Introduction

Picture this: You walk into your classroom and your teacher tells you there's going to be a test. She wants you to flap your arms as hard as you can and try to fly from there to the cafeteria. She's going to give a bird the same test. If the bird can fly to the cafeteria but you can't, he or she will pass the test and you won't. Your teacher will conclude that the bird is smarter than you are. Is the test fair? Of course not. Why? Because birds can fly and humans can't.

Humans are only one of the *1.2 million* species of animals (that we know of) on Earth. And each species has unique traits and abilities. But for centuries, humans judged the intelligence of all other animals based on how well they could do the things that *humans* are good at.

For example, researchers came up with a test for an elephant named Kandula. They hung some yummy fruit just out of his reach. Then they gave him a stick to see if he would use it to knock the fruit down, as humans would. But Kandula wasn't interested in using the stick. Was it because he wasn't bright enough to figure out what to do with it? Nope. (As you'll read in this book, elephants use sticks and other tools to accomplish lots of things.) Elephants' trunks have a powerful sense of smell, which helps them locate food high in the trees. Their trunks also have a strong grip as well as sensitive skin that allows them to identify items they can't see, much like human hands. Kandula knew that if he wrapped his trunk around the stick, it would decrease his ability to smell, feel and grab the fruit. Why in the world would he want that thing?

Kandula didn't need to wise up. The scientists did. When they finally gave him a large cube, he immediately rolled it below where the fruit was hanging, boosted himself up, and snatched the tasty treat. When they gave him a tire, he did the same thing. They offered him blocks that were too small to use as stools on their own, so he stacked them on top of each other. They even hid different objects in his habitat. But each time, he gathered the items and used them to make something he could stand on. The scientists were amazed at how easily he could solve each problem.

Like Kandula with that silly stick, most animals didn't act like humans would when early scientists tried various tests. So they incorrectly assumed that all other species were less intelligent than ours. Thankfully, people have started to realize that different kinds of animals are brilliant in different ways.

When humans stop thinking of ourselves as superior to all other animals (which is called "**speciesism**"), we can actually learn a lot from them. The first pilots studied how birds take off, soar through the air and land, and they copied their techniques to develop airplanes. Later, airlines learned how to get passengers on and off planes faster by observing ants, who are masters of cooperation. The idea for drinking straws came from watching butterflies, who insert a long, round part of their mouth into flowers to suck up nectar. Bike helmets are a copy of turtles' protective shells. We have ducks to thank for swim fins, because their webbed feet make them excellent swimmers. Have you hung something on a wall using a suction cup? We didn't think of those either. People (maybe divers wearing swim fins!) just noticed how tightly octopuses could grip objects with the suckers on their arms. This is known as "biomimicry", which describes how humans copy nature to solve problems.

Humans used to think we were the only ones who learned languages, used tools, and formed close-knit families. Now we know that other animals do these things, too. And when other species don't choose to do the same things humans do, like make fires, it doesn't necessarily mean that they can't. It could be that they don't need or want to.

Sometimes the most impressive abilities can be found in the most surprising places. Just look at slime molds. These amoebas live in the soil and are made up of just one cell, but you probably wouldn't guess that if you saw one. They can reproduce and grow to be up to 10 feet long. And they form some astonishing colours and shapes. Slime molds can look like honeycombs or rainbow popsicles. One kind is called "dog vomit"! You can guess what that one looks like. That's not even the most interesting thing about slime molds. They can solve mazes. A slime mold placed at one end of a maze will grow until it can reach food placed at the other end. As it travels, when it reaches a dead end, it turns around and tries again. It identifies paths it has already taken and can reach the end of the maze in just a few hours. If slime molds are this amazing, what about animals?

In this book, we'll take a trip around the world, flying high into the sky, descending deep into the ocean, and trekking far into the forest to learn about the remarkable animals who share this planet with us. We'll discover some of the fascinating capabilities that make each of us who we are. And we just might find that in many ways—such as how we work hard, have fun, and love our families and friends—we're actually not that different after all.

If you see **underlined words**, you can look up their meaning in the glossary at the back of the book. And if some of the facts in this book surprise you and you want to see animals in action, just do a quick internet search: You'll find many amazing animal videos!

Chapter 1

Daring Journeys

Most humans, like you and your family, rely on all kinds of gadgets to travel from one place to another. We type an address into our phones or our grown-up types one into their car's GPS and a voice tells them every turn they need to make. Drivers have red and green lights to tell them when to stop and when it's safe to go, and there are signs on every street and building. And sometimes we still get lost!

One woman in Canada called the police because her car ended up in Lake Huron. She had turned where her GPS told her to, even though the "road" wasn't a road at all—it was a dock over the water. She followed the directions all the way to the end of it and drove her car straight into the lake. Luckily, it wasn't deep at that point. Maybe she should have asked a sea turtle for directions instead!

Sea turtles find their way through vast oceans by orienting themselves along the north-south lines of the Earth's **magnetic field**. This force field is made by the movement of liquid iron in the Earth's centre. If you've ever used a **compass**, you were reading the Earth's magnetic field. But sea turtles don't need a gadget. Their internal compass is so accurate that they can find their way back to the exact beach where they were hatched to lay their own eggs, even many years later and from thousands of miles away.

All animals except humans use only their own wits to get where they're going. And they accomplish some impressive feats.

Have you used a smartwatch to find out how many steps you've taken and how fast you've gone? Well, no one has made a step-counting device small enough for ants yet, but they don't need one. Ants who live in the desert can't look for familiar plants and trees to find their way home, so when they leave the nest, they count their steps. They also keep track of their turns, their speed, and how much time has passed. Then these smart insects use math to figure out the fastest way back.

When animals need to travel long distances, they can't just hop into a car or on a plane or a boat. They have to depend on their own strength and endurance. Do you get tired after running for a few minutes? Small white birds called Arctic terns would fit in the palm of your hand, but they fly all the way from the North Pole to the South Pole every year. That's over 20,000 kilometres! Arctic terns hold the world record for the longest annual **migration**. Out of all the animals who move to a different area of the world for part of each year (usually because of weather), these tiny, tough birds go the farthest.

Many other animals are making their own amazing voyages all around us all the time.

Taking to the Skies

Klepetan and Malena are two beautiful storks. They live together on a rooftop in a small village in Croatia. Like a lot of birds, storks choose only one mate, and this couple has been "married" for most of their lives. Also like a lot of birds, they fly south for the winter and come home in the spring. Well, Klepetan does. Couples normally make the trip together, but Malena was shot by a hunter and can't fly anymore. The man who takes care of her brings her inside during cold weather. She waits with him while Klepetan makes the 8,000-kilometre trip to South Africa. He stays in his wintering spot with the other storks, and on the exact same day every spring, he returns to the same roof to see Malena.

Scientists aren't sure how birds are able to make such long trips to such specific locations, but they have a few ideas. Brainy birds might read the Earth's magnetic field. Some might use the sun and stars to create a giant sky map. And pigeons may create "sound maps" of areas that help them "hear" their way home. Pigeons are so skilled that in the past, humans used them to carry important messages. During World War I, a clever pigeon named Cher Ami even saved the lives of 194 American soldiers who had been separated from the rest of the troops. Cher Ami flew 40 kilometres in just 25 minutes to carry a message to the people who could rescue them. He continued flying even after being shot twice. He was given an award, and there's an exhibit honouring

DID YOU KNOW?

People who study fish say that they can feel pain, just like any other animals. Fish have more than 20 **pain receptors** in their mouths and heads. When their lips touched irritating chemicals, they rubbed their mouths against the tank walls, just like we rub our knees when we bump them. Researchers have also discovered that fish can talk to each other, use tools and recognize themselves in a mirror. Some even sing!

him in the National Museum of American History in Washington, D.C. Now we can send messages using much better ways that don't ruffle any feathers.

Braving the Seas

Oceans cover more than two-thirds of the Earth's surface. If you've ever been swimming in one, you know that the water starts to get dark at just a few feet deep. But ocean animals easily glide around their large watery home, even in the deepest, darkest parts. Many of them travel hundreds or thousands of miles a year. Western gray whales (who can grow to 50 feet long) travel up to 16,000 kilometres a year. Their babies are born in the warm waters near the **equator**. When the babies are old enough, the whales swim all the way to the Arctic or Antarctic oceans, which are full of food. That would be like if you swam from Mexico to Russia!

Pacific salmon don't swim as far, but their journey is still extraordinary. These fish hatch in freshwater streams in the Northwest region of the U.S. They adapt to saltwater and head out into the ocean to find food and grow larger and stronger. They need to get as big and muscular as they can over the following few years, because the trip back home to build their nests and lay eggs will be a tough one.

Rivers flow into the ocean, so to return home, Pacific salmon have to fight *against* the current the whole way. Their journey is often several hundred kilometres long. They dash *up* river rapids and even *up* waterfalls, leaping as high as 12 feet into the air. And they have to dodge predators, including bears, eagles and humans. Scientists don't know exactly how they find the same stream they hatched in. They might read the Earth's magnetic field or use their exceptional sense of smell to guide them back to familiar territory.

Tiny Trips

Even the smallest animals can achieve big things. Bees can return to their hives even after being trapped inside a car and driven miles away. (But if you find a bee in your car, please be kind and let them out.) Humans don't know how they do this, but they may use landmarks or the position of the sun.

Other insects find their way by looking at the stars. Dung beetles are insects who eat poop. At night, they shape poop into balls and roll the balls home. They can move more than 1,100 times their own weight. That would be the same as a human pulling six double-decker buses! If other bugs try to steal part of a ball, the dung beetles have to shoo them away. And that can get them turned around. To get going in the right direction again, they climb on top of the balls and do something that looks like dancing. What they're really doing is studying the stars, which helps them find their way home.

Animals don't even need legs, wings, or fins to get them home. A woman named Ruth who lives in England was upset because her garden was full of snails. They were eating her lettuce, beans, flowers—anything that looked tasty. She didn't want to harm them, so she moved them to the nearby forest. But a few days later, the snails (who can only move so fast, after all) were back. Ruth tried again and again. But no matter where she moved the snails, they always came back to her garden. She was fascinated. She started learning more about these animals and even wrote a book about them. And she realized that even for snails, there's no place like home.

Lumbering on Land

Unlike other animals you've read about, elephants aren't born knowing how to find their way from place to place. They have to learn. And for that, they depend on the oldest and wisest female in their herd, the **matriarch**. She leads them through the safest routes and to the most reliable places to find food and water. Some African elephants live in deserts that get only four inches of rain a year. The herd's survival depends on the matriarch's memory. When water has run out, matriarchs have led their herds to faraway watering holes that they hadn't been to in 30 years.

Humans have watched elephant matriarchs teach their herds another trick to find water. Rivers in the desert are dry for most of the year. But these smart animals know that sometimes there's water just below the riverbed. They use their trunks and legs to dig until the water comes to the surface. Smaller animals rush to join the elephants in getting a drink!

You've probably heard of the World Cup, the world's largest soccer tournament. But have you heard of the World Cup of Wildlife? It's also called The Great Migration, and it's the largest migration of land animals on Earth. Each year, 200,000 zebras, 400,000 gazelles and more than 1.5 million wildebeests make an 800-kilometre trek in a giant circle. They follow the seasonal rains as they fall on the eastern coast of Africa to eat the lush green grass. Most of the migration occurs in the Serengeti, a large natural area that has forests, plains, rivers, hills and swamps.

Wildebeests all have their babies within a few weeks of each other in January or February. (If you remember the movie *The Lion King*, you know what wildebeests look like.) The babies are on their feet and walking within a few minutes of birth! They have to be ready for the long trip ahead of them.

As the ground in the southern Serengeti dries out, this large group of animals moves west. Throughout

KIND KIDS

Janeysha and her brother were playing outside when they heard meowing from inside a storm drain. They ran to ask their mom to call emergency services. Firefighters arrived and quickly took the cover off the drain, but none of them could fit inside. Janeysha bravely asked the firefighters to lower *her* down the drain instead. When they pulled her back up, she was holding a scared, hungry, grateful kitten! The firefighters took the kitten to the animal shelter, and soon Stormy (as she was later named) had a family to keep her safe inside.

the year, they work their way north, then east, then back south, moving with the rainfall. They face many obstacles along the way. They have to swim across raging rivers and are chased by lions, hyenas, leopards, and cheetahs. The younger members of the herd must learn from the older members about which way to go and how to stay safe. The herd makes it back to the southern Serengeti around November, and The Great Migration starts all over again.

Our cats and dogs don't need to learn large areas by heart. It's our job to keep them protected inside and give them everything they need. But cats and dogs who've gotten lost have known to travel long distances to get back home.

A couple named Jacob and Bonnie took a trip in their RV. They left their home in Florida and went up the coast about 320 kilometres. When they arrived, their cat, Holly, escaped from the camper and disappeared. They searched for her for days but finally had to return home. Jacob and Bonnie were heartbroken. Then, two months later, they got a phone call. Holly was in a neighbour's yard just a few blocks away! She had found her way back to her family.

A dog named Bobbie traveled 4,500 kilometres to get back to his family! He had gotten lost during a family trip. He spent six months working his way back to his home in Oregon and was then known as "Bobbie the Wonder Dog".

So how did they do it? Again, animals are much better at sensing the Earth's electromagnetic field than humans are. But cats and dogs also rely on their noses. Dogs' sense of smell is so powerful that they can pick up scents *and* pinpoint their location. This allows them to create detailed "scent maps" of their worlds. When you're taking a dog for a walk, give them time to sniff. Smelling is the main way they take in information, and it could help them get back home if they ever get lost.

Humans will probably never fully understand how animals make such remarkable journeys. But we do know that they're smart, capable and determined.

WHAT DO YOU THINK?

Which animals have you seen, and where do you think they might have been going?

If you ever see kids stomping on ants or snails or throwing things at birds, ask them to stop and think about where these animals might be going and how hard they're working to get there. You can tell them what you've learned from this book: Animals are amazing and deserve to be treated with kindness. In order to help animals on their journeys, some people pick up litter or plant flowers and shrubs that provide food. What could you do to help?

What are some things humans do that makes it harder for animals to get to where they need to go?

Chapter 2
Animal Voices

Do you ever talk to animals and wish they could talk to you? Many people do. Maybe that's why some of our favourite books and movies include animals, like *Charlotte's Web, The Little Mermaid, The Jungle Book, Finding Nemo* and *Ferdinand.* They help us imagine what animals might be thinking and what they might tell us if they could talk.

It may make you happy to know that animals *do* talk. They speak their own languages, just as humans living in different parts of the world speak different languages. They also use gestures and body language to communicate, just like us. Do you argue with your siblings about who gets the first piece of cake or who gets to sit by the car window? Bats argue with their siblings, too. Scientists studied Egyptian fruit bats' squeaks. They learned that the tiny animals quarrel over pieces of fruit and perching spots on a cave wall.

Chimpanzees communicate using body language, including gestures and facial expressions. And a lot of their gestures look similar to ones humans use. Do you hold out your palm to ask for something? Chimpanzees do, too. They also push away with their hand to say, "Go away". And chimpanzee mothers extend an arm to their young to invite them onto their laps.

Do you remember how Cinderella's mouse friends

DID YOU KNOW?

People who have had mice companions know that they're affectionate and intelligent. They love to cuddle, and they form close bonds with their families and their human guardians. Mice even enjoy getting gentle massages. And they'll lovingly try to "**groom**" (clean) human fingers by licking them. Curious mice have fun solving puzzles that contain treats, and they like to go exploring. When wild mice accidentally come into our homes, we can be kind by using **humane live traps** to help them get back outside.

liked to sing and dance? Real mice sing too, but in pitches that are too high for human ears to hear. Using special microphones, we've been able to hear them singing sweet songs to each other. Boy mice especially enjoy singing to impress girl mice.

Almost anywhere you look, animals are having conversations. And what they're talking about might surprise you.

Woof, Meow, and Wow!

If you've spent time with a dog, you know that dogs understand a lot of human words. Sometimes we even have to spell words such as *w-a-l-k* and *t-r-e-a-t* so they *won't* know what we're saying! Most dogs learn almost 200 human words. And our canine companions don't just notice *what* we say—they also pick up on *how* we say it. Dogs love it when their humans speak sweetly to them and praise them with words such as "good boy" or "well done".

Do you sometimes think your dog can tell when you're having a bad day? You're probably right. Dogs can read emotions on people's faces and appear to feel sympathy for us when we're upset.

Dogs are much better at learning our

language than we are at learning theirs. But scientists do know that they make many different sounds and that each one has its own meaning. Dogs use particular barks, yaps, whines, howls, and growls to communicate. They use one kind of growl to say, “Stay away from my food”. Another kind of growl means “Here comes a stranger”. These growls might sound the same to us but not to other dogs.

Some dogs have been given the chance to use human words to talk to us. A woman named Christina works with children who need help with speech. She has a special keyboard with buttons on it that each play one word. Christina wanted to know if her dog, Stella, could also use the keyboard. Stella quickly learned to press buttons to say, “water”, “play”, and “outside”. Then she started learning more words. Once, Christina forgot to give Stella her dinner. So, Stella reminded her by pressing the buttons for “eat” and “no”.

One day, Christina was talking on the phone. Stella wanted her attention. She pushed the “look”, “come”, “play” buttons. Christina kept talking. Stella tried again. “Want. Play. Outside.” Christina was still on the phone. Stella got frustrated and did something funny. She went to her keyboard and pressed the buttons for “love you” and “no”!

We can make sure our dogs always think, “love you” and “yes”! We can keep them safe inside, always remember to give them food and water, play with them, and take them for walks.

Do you live with a cat? They probably have a name for you. People who study cats learned that they create specific meows to name their guardians. Your cat might expect you to come when they call you! Does your cat rub against your legs or wrap their tail around you? That's how they say "hello" and give you a hug.

If you want to try speaking your cat's language, try blinking slowly at them. They may even do it back. Slow blinking is how cats smile at us. Some vets think it can even be a way to say, "I love you". Cats can also tell when we're upset. Rubbing their head against us is how they offer comfort. And veterinarians say that cats do know their names—even if they ignore you!

Frogs and toads have more in common with dogs and cats than you may think. They use many different sounds, and certain species have their very own sounds. They use whistles, chirps, croaks, ribbits, clucks, peeps, grunts and even barks. Brazilian torrent frogs have lots of ways of getting their message across. In addition to making plenty of noise, they bob their heads and wave their legs. These frogs even dance! Males shake their feet, bounce their heads and shimmy around to get females' attention. They also dance to scare off predators and to warn other frogs of danger.

Deep-Sea Communication

Just as each human has their own name, each dolphin

has their own call. When one dolphin gives their distinct whistle, the rest of the pod knows who's speaking. They can also recognize the whistles of friends they haven't seen in 20 years. And they respond when someone calls their "name" (or whistle), too.

Human ears can sometimes hear dolphins' whistles. But we can only hear many of the sounds they make with special underwater equipment. When scientists studied these sounds, they found that dolphins' speech patterns are a lot like ours, which means that even though the words we say are different, we say them in a similar way. Dolphins string together complex words and sentences. They even pause and take turns speaking, just like us.

Blue whales are the largest animals who have ever existed. They can grow to nearly 100 feet long and weigh upto 170 tonnes. And these massive animals have booming voices to match their size. The opposite of dolphins' sounds, blue whales' calls are too *low* for human ears to hear. But they can hear each other, even across hundreds of kilometres. Blue whales can be an ocean apart and find each other by using their voices.

The voices of smaller humpback whales are

KIND KIDS

Middle school student Alayna was upset when she learned that frogs are taken from their homes in nature to be **dissected** in classrooms. With help from her mom and TeachKind, she gave her school a special present. TeachKind donated **SynFrogs**, which look and feel like real frogs but are actually lifelike models. Students can use them to learn, keeping real frogs *hoppy*!

notable for a different reason: These animals love to sing. Male humpbacks might sing for hours at a time. They can produce songs that are so complex that it takes a trained musician to truly appreciate them.

Some fish SHOUT! Little minnows called blacktail shiners usually use their “indoor voice”. But when noisy cars rumble across a bridge or boats with loud motors zip by, they speak up to be heard. Do you cup your hands around your mouth so people who are far away can hear you? You're acting like a pearlfish! These small, see-through fish use oyster shells to amp up their volume.

For years, people who lived on houseboats near a town in California tried to figure out what was making the loud noise they kept hearing. They complained to the town that the whirring sound was waking them up at night. But what was it? Machines? Water pumps? Submarines? Finally, researchers found out where the noise was coming from. Silvery plainfin midshipman fish were humming loudly! The boaters knew that they needed to let them sing. (But some might have asked them to please keep it down at night.)

Songs in the Sky

Have you ever listened to birds singing and thought their songs sounded pretty? These melodies are actually more than pretty—they're also useful. Birds sing to share information with their partners, young, and flockmates. Some birds are born knowing how to sing, but others have to learn. The way they do this is similar to how humans learn to talk. For several species of songbirds, the males serve as teachers and hold "song schools" for the young birds. The teachers sing slowly and repeat the notes to help their students catch on. When baby songbirds are learning to sing, their songs sound like gibberish, like a human baby trying to talk. They have to practice to keep getting better.

Humans can only hear all the notes birds sing by recording the songs and playing them slowly. Researchers who have done that have heard how intricate some songs are. They can even sound similar to orchestral music.

Remember how blacktail shiners raise their voices when they need to so other fish can hear them? Birds sometimes raise their voices, too. Those who live in noisy cities still need to communicate with each other about important things. They've learned to sing higher notes to be heard above the ruckus.

Sometimes the things birds say to each other can be lovey-dovey. Barn owls typically stay together for life. But first, they have to find the right partner. When a barn owl notices someone they think is cute, they make special sounds to show their interest. Sandhill cranes, with their long necks and even longer legs, do something similar. Couples express their love for each other by making sweet calls in unison.

Like dolphins, when songbirds have a conversation,

DID YOU KNOW?

You may be learning about **idioms** in school. These are phrases that mean something different than the actual words do. For example, if someone is "beating around the bush", they're avoiding talking about something important. But some of the idioms people use can be unkind to animals. Instead of "kill two birds with one stone", try using "feed two birds with one scone". You can replace "let the cat out of the bag" with "spill the beans". And "be the guinea pig" can become "be the test tube". It's also not accurate to call an animal "it". "It" refers to an object, not a living, feeling being. Instead, try using "he", "she", or "they".

they let each other finish chirping before chiming in. And some bird species don't tolerate impolite interruptions. If you're talking to a black-capped chickadee or a European starling, remember to wait your turn. Otherwise, they might give you the silent treatment or fly away! You also never want to get on a crow's bad side. If you wrong them, they'll tell their entire flock about it—and the group will remember your face for years.

While many animals can *understand* human words, some bird species teach themselves to *say* them. Cockatoos, white birds with tall feather "hats," memorize conversations and repeat them back, mimicking both sides. Brightly coloured parrots have been known to speak multiple languages.

But a team of scientists realized that birds who live in people's homes are often lonely. They wanted to find out if these birds would enjoy video calls with other birds to chat. The researchers taught a group of lonesome parrots to make video calls by tapping another bird's picture. The parrots never wanted to get off the phone! They made friends, sang and danced together, and showed each other their toys. One bird even taught another how to fly. And they didn't like it when their screen time was up, just like many of us. Although they did all these things, birds would rather live with their flocks in their natural habitat, where they can fly and play together.

Hitting the Books

Other animals have learned how to read. Researchers showed a group of horses three different signs. They demonstrated how one sign meant that a horse wanted a warm blanket placed on their back. Another sign meant that they wanted the blanket removed. The last sign meant "no changes". After just a few days, the horses started telling their caregivers what they wanted by touching the correct sign.

An elephant named Donna was shown several different pictures. She was able to recognize her favourite food, a banana. When she touched the picture of the banana, her caregivers gave her bananas. So you can probably guess what happened next: She started pressing the button all the time!

Animals may not always speak in ways we can easily understand. But they exchange information with each other constantly. Almost anywhere we are, we can hear their beautiful, mysterious languages.

WHAT DO YOU THINK?

What else do you think animals talk about? If we could understand their languages better, what do you think they would tell us? Do you think they might ask us to be kind and not do things that hurt them or make them feel bad?

Chapter 3

Love and Friendship

Wounda the chimpanzee was very sick. She wasn't able to forage for food and was getting weaker. Luckily, kind people found her in the forest in Central Africa and took her to the chimpanzee rescue center, which had been started by a researcher named Jane Goodall. Jane loved chimpanzees and was working to help them. For two years, she and the other workers at the center took care of Wounda. They gave her medicine and food and helped her get stronger.

Finally, she was healthy enough to live on her own. Jane and her team took Wounda to a nearby island. It was an **animal sanctuary**—a place where animals are protected but still free to roam and explore. Wounda climbed on top of her travel carrier and looked around at her lovely new home. She could probably hear the sounds of the other rescued chimpanzees who would be her friends. But she didn't run off to discover all the wonderful things that were waiting. Instead, she threw her arms around Jane. She held her close and hugged her for a long time. Jane hugged back. Wounda knew that it was time to go, but she couldn't leave without thanking the woman who had saved her life. And to the millions of people who watched the viral video, it looked like Wounda was saying, "I love you".

Love Isn't Just for Humans

Sometimes, animals show love much like we do. Other times, it can look a little different. Has a dog ever licked your hands and face? We would probably laugh and run away if a human tried to do this. But we know that's how dogs give kisses. No matter how animals choose to say, "I love you", one thing is for certain: Their love is sincere.

True Friends

Elephants use their trunks to show affection. They give gentle pats and rubs and wrap their trunks together just like humans join hands. They even compete in friendly games of trunk wrestling!

Tarra is an Asian elephant who was taken from her home and family when she was only 6 months old. She wasn't allowed to play and was forced to perform in circuses, at amusement parks, and on television. But then her caretaker realized that this isn't the way animals should be treated. She wanted to do what was best for Tarra and started an elephant sanctuary. Tarra was delighted. She could roam hundreds of acres of land and forests that mimicked her natural home in Asia. She munched on watermelons and even swam across a 25-acre pond using her trunk like a snorkel. Best of all, Tarra got to make friends. She finally had a herd of elephant buddies just as she would have had in nature. And soon Tarra had picked her best friend. But she wasn't another elephant. A stray dog named Bella had walked into the sanctuary, and she and Tarra liked each other instantly. Bella stayed, and the new friends went for long walks, played, ate together and slept next to each other. Tarra would even pet Bella with her trunk and give her soft tummy rubs with her huge foot.

One day, Bella got injured. Workers took her to the sanctuary's office, where they would take care of her. For weeks, Tarra stayed outside the building and kept an eye on her friend. Caregivers carried Bella outside every day so they could see each other. And as soon as Bella healed, she darted outside to see Tarra. The two friends ran off to discover their next adventure.

Crows form close friendships, too—sometimes even with humans. Remember how crows memorize the faces of humans they don't like? This works both ways. They also learn the faces of people who treat them kindly. A flock of crows in the US liked a girl named Gabi so much that they started bringing her presents. They gave her beads, bottle caps, pennies, paper clips—anything the birds found that they

KIND KIDS

Aravind Valliyate was a grade 11 student at Step by Step School, Noida, when he and other students personally submitted copies of a petition with signatures of 1,00,000 students from schools across the country urging the Indian Ministry of Fisheries, Animal Husbandry and Dairying to pass draft rules to prohibit the use of animals in circuses. These students knew their animal friends want to live in loving homes or with their families in their jungle homes, not be forced to perform tricks. These days, circuses are increasingly using robot animals instead.

thought she would like. One day, Gabi's mother, a photographer, lost the lens cap to her camera in an alley near their home. But the family's crow friends spotted it. They picked up the lens cap, carried it back, rinsed it off in a birdbath, and placed it on the edge to dry.

Finding Someone Special

Animals may not write love notes or go to the movies, but they *do* try to impress each other.

Some men drive flashy sports cars to get attention, but male Japanese puffer fish have them beat. These fish create extraordinary pieces of artwork on the sea floor. They vigorously flap their fins to carve pretty circular patterns into the sand. Puffers are only about 5 inches long, so it can take 10 days for them to finish their masterpieces, which can measure 7 feet in diameter. To make the artwork even more special, puffer fish decorate the circles with shells and pieces of coral. Then, they wait for females to swim by so they can show off their handiwork.

Have you ever seen a couple get engaged with a diamond ring? Adélie penguins use pebbles. They live in Antarctica, which is covered with ice and snow. Small rocks can create a nest that's a little warmer, but they're hard to find. A male Adélie penguin will spend days searching for pebbles to make a nest. When he's finished, he excitedly points out the nest to females to prove that he would be a great partner and dad. If a female likes him, they bow to each other, just like you might bow after performing in a play. Adélie penguin couples often stay together for the rest of their lives.

Male barn owls also try to win over females they like by bringing them little gifts. And when southern right whales are "dating", they touch their flippers together softly. Bald eagle couples like to hold **talons** as they flip and spin through the sky, and seahorses hold tails.

Making It Last

Do you know people who have been married for a long time? Many animals make a lifetime commitment, too. Pairs of prairie voles (tiny rodents who look like mice) are very devoted to each other. Couples like to spend as much time together as possible, and they're champion snugglers. They comfort each other when they're stressed, offering lots of hugs and kisses. They always try to cooperate and work together.

Do you like to dance? So do Laysan albatrosses. These tall, elegant "tuxedo" birds care deeply about their mates. Couples dance together on their "anniversaries" every year—and this may be for up to 50 years! Macaroni penguins dance with their sweeties, too. When these lovebirds see each other after being apart, they do a happy dance. Atlantic puffin birds, with their black-and-white feathers, look similar to Laysan albatrosses or penguins.

Dedicated puffin couples are just as mushy. They nuzzle their beaks together to show that they care.

Some lizards have long-lasting relationships, too. Shingleback skinks are scaly lizards who are about as long as your forearm. Male skinks often softly pat their female companions, and couples like to get as close as they can while they're walking.

Not only do graceful gray wolves stay with their partners for life, they also stay with their whole family. When a pair has pups, the entire pack pitches in to help. Coyotes, their close relatives, are just as loyal. Researchers who studied these wild dogs learned that dynamic duos stick together in good times and bad.

Sharing Hard Times

Everyone goes through tough times. It's hard when we get injured or sick, a friend moves, somebody is unkind, or someone we love passes away. It may help to know that *all* of us feel sad when bad things happen. But we can count on our families and friends to be there for us—and animals can, too. Just like humans, animals have **empathy**, which means that they can put themselves in someone else's place and understand how they feel. They recognize when someone is hurting and often try to help even if it may cause them harm.

In California, forests were quickly being burned

by a raging wildfire. One stallion (a male horse) was being loaded into a trailer to be taken to safety when he stopped short. He stuck up his ears and turned his head. He heard something that humans couldn't. Somewhere in the distance, a mare (a female horse) was crying out. The stallion broke away and galloped off through the smoke. A few minutes later, he returned—and he wasn't alone. He had found the mare and her filly (a young female horse) and led them out so they could be rescued, too. Have you ever seen a movie in which a brave firefighter darts into a building to save people's lives? Now you know that animals also risk their lives to save others.

Rats care deeply about others. A long time ago, a scientist put two rats in boxes next to each other for a cruel experiment. He trained one of the rats to push a lever to get food. Then he changed the outcome. When the rat pushed the lever, he still received his food—but his neighbour got a shock. The mean scientist was in for a surprise: These kind rats showed him that they would rather go without food than give someone else a shock. When the same experiment was performed on rhesus monkeys, they reacted the same way. They refused to hurt anyone else, even to get what they wanted. Humans should be as kind as animals are

KIND KIDS

After large wildfires in Australia destroyed many animals' homes, students and teachers at a secondary school in Maine jumped into action. They 3D-printed **looms** to weave with and accepted donations of yarn. They made cozy nests, blankets, and pouches for the animals. The students said that they also wanted to help *all* animals by being kind to them.

DID YOU KNOW?

Did you know that cats often injure and kill birds and other wildlife? We can keep wild animals safe by keeping an eye on companion cats, training them to walk on a harness, or letting them explore the outdoors in a large, netted area. All of this is safer for cats too, who often get hit by cars. We can also be kind to birds by putting out clean water bowls. And we can plant trees, flowers and plants that provide habitat and food.

and not experiment on *any* of them.

Have you ever had an argument with a friend? Pigs disagree sometimes, too. And when two pigs get upset with each other, a third pig will often show them empathy and try to calm things down. The third pig will softly touch snouts with a warring pig or stroke them with their ears. The pigs will cool off and come to an agreement. Wolves and birds also use this tactic.

When an elephant is distressed, in addition to giving trunk rubs, members of their herd form a protective circle around them and say soothing things to reassure them. When an elephant passes away, their herd holds a funeral. An African elephant named Eleanor was the matriarch of her herd. She was getting older and had been sick for some time. When Eleanor was too weak to keep walking, her family and friends gathered around her, sweetly stroking her with their trunks. After she passed away, more elephants came. They petted her body, saying their goodbyes. Over the next few days, elephants from separate, unrelated families came to pay their respects, too. Elephants will often find a pretty spot with a cushion of brush to lay their loved one to rest.

Flocks of crows also find it comforting to hold funerals. When a crow passes away, their flockmates huddle around them for several hours. They frequently give the fallen bird a respectful burial, placing sticks or other items on top of them.

Geese are very loyal birds. They stay with their chosen partner for life. When a goose's mate passes away, the surviving partner spends time alone to mourn. Some choose never to have another partner. In 2016, viral pictures touched hearts around the world. A female goose in China had been wrapped up on the back of a motorcycle and was being taken away to be killed for food. Another goose, her longtime partner, stood beside her crying out and trying to help her. Craning their necks, they "kissed" each other one last time. People who saw the photos could tell that the geese felt emotional pain over the loss of their partner.

Cows frequently shed tears just like we do when they experience a loss. On dairy farms, farmers take cows' babies away from them so that humans can drink the mothers' milk. The mothers and babies cry and call for each other for days. A cow named Clarabelle was rescued by an animal sanctuary. When she got there, volunteers were excited to see that she was going to have a baby. They took good care of Clarabelle and got everything ready for her little one.

But then Clarabelle started acting strangely. She was avoiding her new friends and sneaking away from the sanctuary. After a search, the volunteers discovered why. Clarabelle's baby had arrived. And since her other calves had been taken away from her, she hid this calf in a tall patch of grass nearby. She kept returning to the sanctuary so people wouldn't suspect anything. But she didn't have to worry—she and her baby were now safe with people who loved them. Clarabelle got to kiss, nuzzle and play with her baby. And they were never apart again.

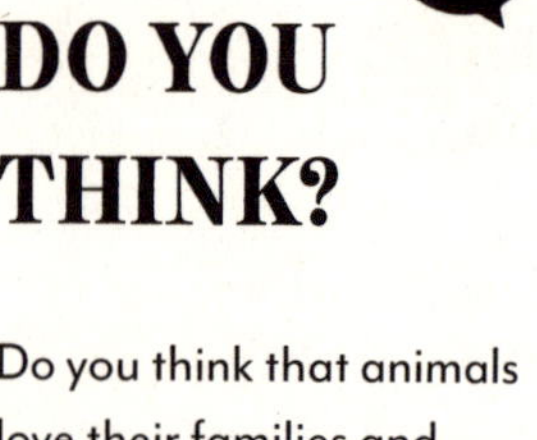

WHAT DO YOU THINK?

Do you think that animals love their families and friends as much as we love ours? Do you show love in some of the same ways they do? Now that you've learned how animals care for and love one another, if someone were to say you were "acting like an animal", would you take it as a compliment?

How have you shown love towards animals? Write below!

Chapter 4
Family First

When you hear words like "love" and "family", do you think of slimy, bloodsucking leeches? Probably not. But even though your aunt might not send you a sweet card with pictures of leeches on it anytime soon, these flat worms are caring family members. Leech grown-ups take great care of their young as they grow. They shuttle them from one safe place to another to protect them from danger.

Other small animals demonstrate big love, too. Wolf spiders carry their unhatched babies in pouches, like wearing a backpack. Once the spiderlings hatch from their sac, they nestle into the hair on their mother's back until they're big enough to live on their own. Even while the mothers are running and jumping, they defend their babies.

But when it comes to which little animals make the biggest display of love, the winners might just be exploding ants. Tree-dwelling ants in the jungles of Southeast Asia have the scientific name *Colobopsis explodens* for a good reason. They have sacs on their bodies that hold poisonous yellow goo. When an intruder tries to attack their colony, the ants defend it with their lives: They make themselves explode, spraying the invader with the sticky, icky fluid and saving the day. The next time someone you love asks you to help out around the house by picking up your clothes or doing the dishes, just remember: At least they didn't ask you to explode!

Other animals show their families that they care in ways that aren't quite as messy but definitely just as impressive.

The Talk of the Farm

Christmas Bonnet, the cow, lives on a pretty farm in England with her herd, made up of family and friends. One day, the farm's owner, Rosamund, moved all the cows with babies to another field so that the government could count them. That left Christmas Bonnet alone. The next day, when Rosamund came to feed her, Christmas Bonnet glared. Rosamund knew she wasn't happy. She apologized and promised that the herd would be together soon. But Christmas Bonnet didn't like waiting. When Rosamund left, the smart cow figured out how to let herself out of her pen. She crossed the farm, going around hedges, gates and fences. Soon, she was happily reunited with her family.

Mr. Rooster is—you guessed it—a rooster, who lives in California. His family includes chickens, dogs and his human guardians, and he loves them all. The chickens like to eat grapes from the family's grapevines. But before Mr. Rooster takes any for himself, he pulls the tall vines down so that the hens, who are shorter, can get a snack. He also hops on top of the shed to be a lookout for the family. And when a car pulls into the driveway, he joins the dogs in running down to inspect the visitor.

Chickens use more than 30 "words" to describe possible threats and whether they're coming by land or the sky. Mother hens start teaching their chicks these and other words while they're still inside their shells. The mothers softly cluck, and the unhatched chicks chirp back!

Baby turkeys start talking to their mother from inside their eggs, too. After they hatch, if a baby gets separated from their mom, they know how to call for her. When the mother bird answers, the baby excitedly flaps their wings and races back to the family.

Pig moms teach their babies in a similar way. They sing to their newborns, which comforts the piglets and helps them learn to communicate. When the piglets are old enough to explore, they still come running when they hear their mothers' voices. Pigs also run to the sound of a pig in distress. Many have even saved their family members' lives.

A pig named Prudence was just 4 months old when she saved her human's life. Dee and Prudence live on a farm, and one day,

DID YOU KNOW?

Pigs enjoy listening to music, playing with footballs and getting massages. They can even play video games!

KIND KIDS

One year, just ahead of World Environment Day, vegan children got dressed up chick and calf costumes in Bengaluru and joined a PETA India awareness program with their parents. Vegans are vegetarians who only eat plant foods. People choose to be vegan for different reasons—some to help animals, others to improve their health, and yet others because growing plant foods is kinder to the planet compared to producing food made from animals.

Dee stepped into deep mud and started sinking. She had a rope in her hand, which she looped around Prudence. Prudence tugged and tugged until Dee was free.

JoAnn, the guardian of a pig named Lulu, suddenly got very sick. Thinking quickly, Lulu broke out of the yard, scraping and cutting her skin on the fence. She dashed into the road and lay down to block traffic, putting her own life in danger. Some people drove around her, but one kind man stopped. When he shouted that he needed help for an injured pig, JoAnn shouted back for help. He called an ambulance, which saved JoAnn's life. And brave Lulu got the veterinary care she needed for her cuts and scrapes, along with lots of pets and treats.

A pig named Spammy rescued his calf best friend from a burning shed, and Dumplin the pig chased away burglars. A pig named Mona held onto the leg of an intruder until police arrived, and Lucky the pig saved his humans from a house fire. Pigs go to great lengths for their family members. And they aren't the only ones.

Love Is in the Air

Birds aren't just loyal spouses. They're caring guardians, too. Has a seagull ever tried to take your food at the beach? They might have been raising babies. Seagull couples share parenting duties. They both sit on the eggs, and when the hatchlings arrive, they take turns finding food. (But you should keep your food and politely tell Mr. or Ms. Seagull that human food isn't healthy for them.)

Have your grown-ups ever embarrassed you? Just be glad you're not a seagull. When someone gets too close to a seagull chick, the mom or dad will whack them in the head, poop on them, and vomit on them! It's not pleasant, but it does work.

Pigeon pairs also share responsibility of their little ones. They trade off sitting on the eggs, and both birds even make milk. They produce "**crop milk**" in their digestive systems and place their beaks inside the hatchlings' mouths to feed it to them. Doves, flamingoes, and some species of penguins do this, too.

Only male emperor penguins can make crop milk, but both adults have to work together closely to take care of their family in frigid Antarctica. Penguins need to maintain a lot of insulating body fat to keep warm. After the female spends two months producing and laying her egg, she's hungry! Females leave for a couple of months to eat as much as they can, and the males take over. They each put their egg on top of their feet and cover it with a feathery fold of skin to keep it warm. Males rely on their body fat to survive since they don't get to eat for months, until

KIND KIDS

In India, Beach Please is a youth-led community that transforms beaches, rivers and other polluted spaces into beautiful, clean areas through trash collection. Look up Beach Please on Instagram to see if they are doing a clean up in your area you can join, or start one on your own with friends!

the females return and the chicks hatch. The gals return and swap again so the guys get their turn to fill up. Males feed the babies crop milk, and females bring some of their own food back up in their throat before it's digested and feed it to the babies.

Sandgrouse are small birds who look a lot like pigeons. The males are great dads. When water is scarce, they'll fly as far as 80 kilometres to find some. They soak up as much water as they can in their chest feathers and fly home. Then the baby birds drink from their feathers.

Police officers in Ohio were surprised when a mother goose started pecking on the door of their cruiser. She pecked and pecked until they got out, then she led them to a spot nearby. Her baby was tangled in a balloon string. The officers rushed to free him, and the grateful mom honked in thanks (her own horn, not the car's).

Did you or your siblings go to daycare? Baby bats do, except they might call it "nightcare". Bat moms hunt for food at night, eating up to 600 mosquitoes in an hour. A bunch of moms get together and create one "nursery colony", where they live together. A few adult bats stay behind each night to babysit, and the next night, they trade.

Are you adopted, or do you know someone who is? Animal parents sometimes choose to adopt, too. A kind man in India saw a fallen tree and checked to make sure no animals were hurt. He discovered a baby owlet (a type of small owl) on the ground. Her nest had been destroyed, and her parents were nowhere in sight. He called PETA India's friends at Animal Rahat ("rahat" means "relief" in Hindi) for help. Rescuers put a birdhouse in the next tree to see if the parents might come back. But the scared and possibly injured adults didn't return.

The rescuers knew that a family of Asian barred owlets lived in a nearby town. These birds were the same species as the rescued owlet and had two youngsters of the same age. The team members drove to the family's tree and gently placed the baby in their house. They held their breath as they watched to make sure everything would be OK. The two owlet siblings instantly snuggled up to their new sister, chirping with excitement! When the parents returned, they immediately started feeding her and taking care of her. Before long, the tiny owlet had grown stronger and healthier. And the parents started teaching all three of their precious nestlings how to fly.

An Ocean of Devotion

Where would you guess sea catfish hide their eggs to keep them safe? Under rocks? In **burrows**? In clumps of seaweed? These whiskered fish actually hide them in their mouths! Some other fish use the same trick, including brightly coloured cichlids, needle-like pikeheads, and jawfish (who have very big mouths, just as you'd expect). The moms seal their lips and don't eat until the eggs hatch, which might take longer than a month. Even after the babies start swimming, at the first hint of danger, they rush to their guardians. The young fish jump right back into their mom's, or sometimes, their dad's, mouth!

Do your grown-ups show you how to do things and help you learn? Animal grown-ups do that, too. Lobsters in the wild can live to be more than 100 years old, and they pass down knowledge from one generation to the next. Orcas live in close family pods, and older relatives help educate the young calves. After a calf is born, their mother guides them to the surface to take their first breath. The mom and other relatives teach the calf the whistles and clicks they'll use to communicate, show them how to hunt for food and teach them everything else they should know. All female orcas and many males stay with their families their whole lives. Although you may have heard these black-and-white beauties being called "killer whales", they're actually a type of dolphin. And they've never hurt a human in the wild. But these brilliant animals have *saved* several people's lives.

The award for the best homemaker under the water might go to bromeliad crabs. Their houses are already pretty. They live in pockets of rainwater inside colourful bromeliad flowers. Adult crabs work hard to keep their homes clean and comfortable for their offspring. Scientists have watched them clear out dirt and things that don't belong and move the water around to add oxygen to it. The crabs even find empty snail shells to bring home. Why? The shells are full of calcium, which makes the water healthier.

Crabs live by the saying "Love your neighbour". If an intruder tries to take over a male Australian fiddler crab's burrow, his neighbour will leave his own burrow to help fight off the trespasser.

When you think about alligators and crocodiles, do you think of them as sweet, caring family members? Maybe not, but you should. Both animals watch over their eggs and nests and defend them from predators. When the hatchlings are ready to emerge, they call out to their mom to let her know. What do you think they say? The mother gently cracks open the eggshells with her teeth and carries the babies into the water. Young alligators and crocodiles live with their mother for months or even years.

Love Exists Deep in the Jungle

Orangutans are **great apes** whose hair colour you can probably guess: orange! They live in rainforests on islands just north of Australia. Orangutan mothers and their babies might have one of the closest bonds in the entire animal kingdom. The mothers only have one baby at a time, and the two of them stay together

WHAT DO YOU THINK?

Which animal family is your favourite? Why? Do you see similarities between animal relatives and your family?

for years. For the first several months, they like to be always touching each other. And after that, they do everything together, like sleeping, playing, and foraging for food (Fruit is their favourite). Even after young orangutans grow up and start their own families, they go back often to visit their moms!

What fun facts about different birds do you know? Write below!

Chapter 5

Let's Get to Work!

Have you ever met a dentist who was a fish? What about a beaver who fights fires? A woodpecker construction worker? A farmer bee? Humans aren't the only ones who do these and many other important jobs.

Cleaner wrasse fish are only about 4 inches long with blue, black, and sometimes yellow stripes. They live in coral reefs and have an interesting career. They clean larger fish's teeth and mouths. They do this by swimming inside and using their own mouths to gently nibble away at anything that shouldn't be there. This provides cleaner wrasses with food and helps the larger fish stay healthy. And in the same way that dentists and hygienists work together in an office, cleaner wrasses set up a group cleaning station. They let "clients" know when it's open by wiggling up and down, kind of like the people who dance near a road with a business's sign to attract passers-by. Larger fish and even turtles line up to have their teeth cleaned. Sometimes the big fish will even spread their fins and gills and ask the cleaner wrasses to give those a touch-up, too.

Can you picture a beaver driving a firetruck or aiming a hose? They may not be able to do those things, but beavers are excellent firefighters. They build dams in streams and rivers to create small ponds where their

KIND KIDS

When actor R. Madhavan's son Vedaant was a child, he won a Compassionate Kid Award from PETA India. That's because instead of collecting gifts, Vedaant would use his birthdays to raise funds for PETA India to help animals.

families live in "beaver lodges". The dams help hold some water in the area as it flows downstream. That creates wetlands that can stop fires from spreading. Wetlands also give animals a safe place during a fire. And the extra water allows more plants to grow, which provides food for many species. The sticks and mud that the dams are made of help clean pollutants out of the water. Beavers work hard to build their dams. If you've ever been called a "busy beaver", now you know what a compliment it is!

Woodpeckers, gophers, and moles don't wear construction hats, but they build a lot of houses. As woodpeckers peck at trees to find insects to eat, they create small hollows that make perfect nests for birds, squirrels and other animals. Gophers and moles dig lots of underground tunnels that serve as shelter for many animals, including foxes, snakes, owls, mice, and rats. When you're standing on grass, you might be on top of an animal apartment complex.

Bees, butterflies, moths, bats, and birds are natural farmers. These animals are called "pollinators", and they help grow a lot of the foods humans eat. They love nutritious nectar and pollen from flowers and must fly from flower to flower gathering it. A single bee may visit 10,000 flowers in a day! Some of the pollen sticks to their bodies, and as they zip around, it gets moved from one plant to another. That helps the plants produce either more beautiful flowers or fruits and veggies. Do you like almonds, apples, avocados, bananas, grapes, pears or strawberries? How about chocolate? (Chocolate comes from cocoa beans.) The next time you see a pollinator, you might want to say, "Thank you". They help create many kinds of food—about one out of every three mouthfuls we eat. When we see them, instead of bothering them or swatting at them, we can let them do their important jobs. And we can move away if we're frightened. Bees don't sting unless *they're* scared of *you*.

While you're doing assignments at school or helping out at home, animals all around the world are also hard at work.

Let's Put Our Heads Together

You've probably watched groups of adults getting together to make decisions. Maybe you've done the same thing with your student council or sports team. Animals hold meetings to discuss important things, too.

Elephant herds talk things over using their voices and gestures. They take turns sharing their thoughts and then choose what will be best for the whole group. When a plan succeeds, elephants celebrate. They lift their heads high, rumble, trumpet and give each other a "high-five" with their trunks.

African wild dogs are sometimes called "painted dogs" because of their colourful orange, white and brown fur. They live in packs in nature, but they do a lot of the same things the dogs you know do, like deciding whether to eat or take a nap. Scientists think these dogs signal to the rest of the pack that they'd like to go look for food by sneezing. Other dogs sneeze if that's what they want to do, too. If they'd rather rest, they don't sneeze. Each sneeze fest ends with a group decision (and, you would think, a lot of tissues).

Tool Time

Have you ever seen a bird holding a stick in their beak? They could have been building a nest, but they might have been using it for another purpose. Wise birds use thin sticks as tools to dig bugs and larvae they want to eat out of tree bark and other tight spaces. The birds even bend the ends of the sticks to make scoops. Some use folded leaves to do the same job, sometimes tearing the edges of the leaf to create a miniature rake.

Birds have even figured out how to use our cars as tools. People in Japan noticed that something funny was happening at a traffic light. Crows were lining up with the people who were getting ready to cross the street. When the cars stopped, the birds darted onto the crosswalk and put walnuts in front of them. Then they raced back to the sidewalk. As the cars drove over the walnuts, they smashed the shells, revealing the tasty nuts inside. When the cars stopped again, the crows would run out and gobble up their treats. If any of the walnuts hadn't broken open, the crows would move them a little and try again.

Seagulls who live near beaches use a different tactic. They like to drop clamshells onto pavements or rocks to break them open. Orange-spotted tuskfish (who are about the length of your arm) do this, too. When they find a buried clam, they flap their gill covers open and shut as fast as they can to blast the sand away. They look like you would if you were doing the chicken dance! They pick the clams up in their mouths and drop them onto rocks until the shell breaks open.

Elephants use tools, too. When an electric fence is blocking their way, they drop rocks and logs on it to **short** it out. They grab sticks to scratch an itch that their trunks can't reach. And they break leafy branches into the perfect shape to swat away flies. Elephants even wash their veggies before eating them. Sometimes they wash their food in water if it's close by. Or they smack plant roots against their feet to get the dirt off. (We don't recommend trying that at home.)

If you often have hair stuck to your shirt, you might get a helping hand from the macaque monkeys who live in parts of Thailand. They like to use strands of human hair as dental floss! They'll also use feathers, grass, or even their own hair to clean their teeth. Dentist cleaner wrasses would be pleased that they're flossing!

Getting the Job Done

Sometimes you don't need tools to get the job done right. You just need brain power and a little effort.

The next time you need help opening a jar, you might want to ask an octopus. They can easily figure out how to take the lids off jars and even off childproof bottles. Then they put their strong arms and suckers to work. Ozy the octopus was taken to an ocean animal hospital in New Zealand with an injured arm. Workers there had a jar of food for him—but he didn't need their help to open it. He unscrewed the lid and was having lunch in under a minute!

Maybe octopuses are so smart because they have one brain in their head and another brain in each arm. That's *nine* brains! These eight-armed geniuses can change the colour and texture of their skin to camouflage themselves as rocks, seaweed, or anything else around them. Some carry empty coconuts or shells with them to use if they need to hide. And they've accomplished many other remarkable feats.

An octopus named Otto let everyone at the aquarium where he was kept in Germany know that he was bored. He entertained himself by juggling, redecorating his tank, and throwing rocks at the tank walls. He also squirted water at the lights, knocking out the lighting for the whole building! Two brainy octopuses figured out how to escape aquariums in New Zealand. Sid kept escaping from his tank and even spent five days hiding in a drain. Finally, the staff recognized that they should set him free. Inky climbed out of his tank, scooted across the floor, and slid down a drainpipe that dropped 164 feet—all the way to the open sea!

Orangutans and cows are brilliant doctors. They know exactly which plants will help when they're feeling sick. If you see a cow nibbling on a willow tree, it's probably because the bark contains a medicine that works like aspirin. Researchers spotted orangutans chewing on leaves of one plant into a lather. They rubbed the ointment they'd made onto their arms or legs for several minutes to relieve pain. Orangutans also construct their own beds each night high up in the trees using just their hands. They expertly weave tree branches together and top them with softer, leafy branches. This creates a strong and comfortable mattress. And they can make one in just five or six minutes!

DID YOU KNOW?

Did you know that almost every animal researchers have observed uses math? A lot of them are better at it than we are. Chickens can add and subtract just three days after they hatch. Silvery green fish called three-spined sticklebacks can glance at a group of about 20 peers and tell the exact number. Some frogs challenge each other to "croak-offs". They go back and forth, correctly adding one croak every time, until they run out of breath. Researchers watched as a black bear counted. They noticed that when items were moving around, he got even *more* accurate.

WHAT DO YOU THINK?

Are some jobs that animals do similar to tasks that you and your family do? Can you think of other ways animals work hard? Were you surprised by the intelligence of any of these amazing animals?

Squirrels are fantastic magicians. They like to hide nuts when no one is watching. But if they catch another squirrel spying, they use a skill called "sleight of hand" to perform a trick. They pretend to bury the nut while quickly switching it from their claw to their mouth. Then they scurry away and bury it in a different location.

Leafcutter ants learned how to farm long before humans did. These miniature gardeners are easy to recognize. You usually see them walking in a line, each carrying a piece of leaf that weighs much more than they do. But the ants don't eat the leaves. They use them to grow a special kind of **fungus** underground. The fungus is full of nutrients and is the ants' most important food. It's so special that you can't find it in nature. Only the ants know how to grow it. Their underground gardens and nests can contain *thousands* of rooms. Imagine having to keep that many rooms clean! Each member of the colony has an important job to do, and they work hard every day.

Can you think of any other fun ways in which animals solve problems? Write below!

Chapter 6

Let's Play!

Scientists were perplexed. They were watching young gorillas do something they'd never seen them do before. One gorilla ran up to another, gave them a gentle tap, and ran away. The second gorilla followed, gave the first one a gentle tap, and ran in the opposite direction. And they kept going. Were these funny animals *playing tag*?

As it turned out, they *were* playing tag. And young gorillas in other groups have been seen doing the same thing. In fact, researchers have learned that most or even all animals like to play, for the same reasons humans do. Playing is fun and can help us learn important skills. For instance, when you're splashing around in a pool or lake, you're learning how to swim, float, and hold your breath. That helps keep you safe in the water. Gorillas who play tag are having a blast while learning how to run, jump, and climb to escape danger.

Playing also helps us learn how to get along with others. Have you ever gotten into an argument over a game? Did your grown-ups or teachers help you and your friend or sibling apologize? Animals sometimes get into disagreements when they play together, too. And learning how to make up helps all of us get better at cooperating.

Having Fun Is Good for Us

You've probably seen kittens wrestling, pouncing on each other, and trading playful swats. And *big* cats do the same thing. YouTube has lots of videos of lions, tigers, jaguars, bobcats and other wild cubs tackling one another, rolling through the grass and romping around. And while all these cats are enjoying themselves, they're also getting stronger and more coordinated. They're learning how to leap and how to land. They're discovering how to defend themselves. Pouncing comes in handy when a piece of food starts to roll away.

These clever cats also know that you don't have to stop having fun just because you grow up. Workers at a sanctuary for rescued big cats in Florida wanted to know what would happen if they gave the adult cats toys to play with. Soon, the workers were laughing so hard their sides hurt. Black panthers and leopards darted in and out of cardboard boxes. Jaguars stalked and attacked laser pointers. A white tiger rolled, chased, and pounced on a big red ball. And rolls of toilet paper ended up all over the fences, the habitats, *and* the cats! These grown-ups clowned around like cubs and reminded the workers to make time for fun.

Baby deer, called fawns, love to race after each other, bouncing and frolicking through fields and forests. They even wag their tails like puppies. And they like to make their moms get in on the fun. They run in circles around their mothers, darting in one direction and then the other. The moms often give in and play, especially because they know that playing chase helps fawns gain strong muscles and quick reflexes. Soon, they'll be able to run up to 72 kilometres an hour and jump almost 9 feet into the air!

Nearby in the forest, baby brown bears are also having a good time. Cubs love to wrestle and play-fight. They stand up on their hind legs and gently paw at and bite each other. And they tumble to the ground, tussle around, and hop back onto their feet again. The babies might not realize it, but they're building muscle and learning how to balance. And that will help them reach leaves and berries, climb trees, and dig dens.

It's Nice to Be Together

Just like humans, animals must learn that it's OK to disagree sometimes. We can still work together and be kind and friendly. Scientists watched one group of pushy macaque monkeys start playing together. As they swung high in the air, ran, and roughhoused together, sometimes they fought. But they also learned that life is better with friends. They got much better at making up and settling their arguments.

Calves need to learn how to live together in a herd and make joint decisions. And when groups of calves are together in a pasture, they have a great time practicing. The whole gang will run, zig and zag, buck, kick up their legs, and twist in the air. They're good at making the group decision that right now is playtime!

It's Party Time!

Many animals play just because they love to.

For example, a favourite game of young meerkats is "sumo wrestler". They teeter on their stubby legs and use their long tails like kickstands as they try to balance. They push and heave and try to knock each other over. When one meerkat wins, they jump onto their opponent's belly and gently nibble at their ears and paws. Sure, they're discovering how to use their bodies and how to get along. But meerkats like to play *a lot*. And they even play outside their den, where it could be dangerous. A scientist named Lynda wanted to know why.

She spent weeks following 45 baby meerkats in South Africa as they grew into adults. She watched as big groups of these little animals would wrestle together, play-bite, and roll on the ground. There would be so many tails, heads, and legs waving around that Lynda couldn't tell what belonged to whom! But she found out the answer to her question: The meerkats played so much just because they wanted to. They were having a good time.

Goats like to get into mischief. They're naturally curious and very good at walking and climbing on steep, rocky, and uneven ground. And that means they have lots of adventures. Many goats confined to pens on farms have figured out how to follow their adventurous spirit. These bright animals study the fences, locks, and latches of their pens to find weak spots. They might let themselves out, or they might just climb the fence. Goats watch each other, and when one figures out a trick to get loose, the others repeat it. And *that* sometimes leads to massive breakouts. On one farm, more than 100 goats broke through a wooden fence and escaped from their enclosure. They had spotted some tasty-looking grass outside some nearby houses and decided to give it a try!

Goats like to explore, have fun, and be happy—and they enjoy being around people who like to do these things, too. If you want to make friends with a goat, try giving them a sweet smile. In one study, researchers showed a group of goats pictures of humans with different expressions. The animals were able to read the emotions on the people's faces. They were much more interested in the ones who were smiling and seemed happy and kind.

Elephants know how to make chores fun. In Africa, where many elephants live, the sun gets very hot. Elephants often travel long distances to find food and water,

KIND KIDS

Twelve-year-old Nirvaan volunteers at an animal sanctuary, helping to care for goats, pigs, cows, and other rescued animals. When a roadside zoo in his hometown flooded, Nirvaan spoke in front of the local government. He explained why the animals there should be in sanctuaries, too. He helped get all of them moved to happy new homes!

and they have to find ways to keep themselves cool. One way they've found is to take mud baths. The cool mud brings their body temperature down, and when it dries, it works like sunscreen. But one big reason why elephants, especially young ones, like to get into mud is to play. They roll around, tackle each other, and slip and slide through the goopy, sticky, entertaining mud.

Many people are surprised to learn that elephants can swim for about 48 kilometres in the ocean without stopping. Like the elephant named Tarra you read about earlier, they use their trunks as snorkels. But they also know that water isn't just for swimming. It's also for running and splashing and playing in the waves, of course.

Sharks also like to have a ball—sometimes with an actual ball. People have spotted sharks bumping their noses into balloons floating on the surface of the water. Some tried to put the balloons in their mouths and shook their heads in amazement when the balloons popped! Sharks play with other objects they find in the water, too. That's one reason why it's important not to litter in the ocean. Sharks need to play with things that are there naturally instead of humans' items that could injure them. Have you ever twirled around holding streamers? Sharks like to flip and spin around in long pieces of seaweed that grow from the ocean floor. They even wrap the seaweed around their noses and swim with it trailing behind them like streamers, while other sharks chase them.

Have you heard of snowboarding? Did you hear about it from a crow? YouTube is full of videos of crows using plastic lids like sleds on snowy roofs. The birds put a lid in their beaks and fly to the top of a roof they like. They set the lid down, hop on with both feet, and slide all the way down. Then they fly their lid back to the top and slide down again. One person also spotted a crow bouncing a rubber ball she had found. And others have seen crows playing tug-of-war with sticks.

Other species of birds like to play, too, and some even make laughing sounds! We know of 65 species of animals who laugh, including foxes, coyotes, orcas, chimpanzees, dolphins, and rats.

While crows are snowboarding, crocodiles are bodysurfing. Some live in saltwater, and their favourite "sport" is using their bodies to surf across ocean waves. Those who live in rivers turn muddy slopes into waterslides. Scientists have also seen crocodiles, alligators, and similar reptiles called caimans playing tag, play-fighting, and giving each other piggyback rides! Crocodiles blow bubbles at each other, too. They also love pink flowers, although people who observe them don't know why. They pick delicate pink flowers and

DID YOU KNOW?

Movies like *Jaws* make sharks out to be vicious, mean human-eaters, but they don't deserve that reputation. Some sharks are even vegetarians! Great white sharks, like those in the movie, rarely attack humans. When they do, it's because they're scared and trying to protect themselves. Humans kill more than 100 million sharks every year, so they have a good reason to be afraid of us. Many species of sharks are now endangered. When we choose not to eat fish, we help save sharks, too. How? When big fishing ships haul in large nets of fish, they also catch sharks and lots of other animals. Not eating fish helps keep all ocean animals safe in the water where they belong!

WHAT DO YOU THINK?

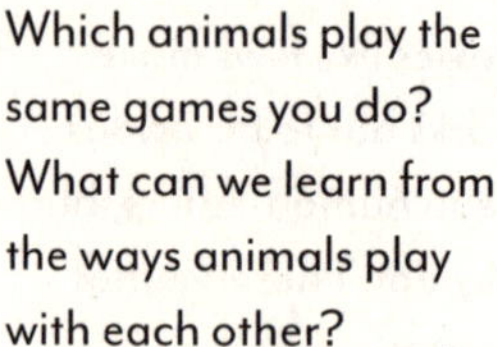

Which animals play the same games you do? What can we learn from the ways animals play with each other?

carefully carry them in their mouths or balance them on the tips of their noses. Maybe crocodiles know that when you have a disagreement with someone, you can bring them flowers to say, "I'm sorry", and make up?

Cool Careers That Help Animals

How would you like to have a cool job helping animals when you grow up? You may dream of being a veterinarian, but that's just one option. You could work in an animal shelter or be a wildlife rehabilitator. You could advocate for animals in court as an animal rights lawyer or run your own sanctuary. And there are lots of exciting jobs that let you combine your compassion for animals with other things you enjoy. If you dream about owning a restaurant, designing clothes, or showing off your skills at writing, painting, building robots, or doing other fun things, find out how you can help animals at the same time!

Shelters Need Helpers

The perfect job for you might be just down the road at your local animal shelter. Shelters take in dogs, cats, rabbits, guinea pigs, mice and other small animals and take care of them while they wait to find their adoptive homes. Shelter workers give them food, water, medicine, baths, toys and playtime and keep them safe and comfortable. They post pictures of the animals online, talk to families who are ready to adopt, and hold fun adoption events and fundraisers. Even if this doesn't become your job one day, you can still volunteer and play a big part in helping animals at shelters.

Would you like to help animals find their permanent homes?

Beat the Bad Guys

Cruelty investigators and animal welfare officers check on animals and find out how they're being treated. They write detailed notes and take pictures and videos of what they find. If people are being unkind, the investigator's evidence can be used to rescue the animals and make sure that those people don't get to be around animals again.

Do you take really good notes, have video camera skills, and want to bring bad guys to justice?

Animals Need Lawyers, Too

An animal lawyer stands up for animals in court. They might work on cases to rescue animals who've been treated badly or help pass laws to protect them.

Can you think of animals who might need a lawyer to help them get out of a bad situation?

Be a Sanctuary Savior

Sanctuaries give animals a spacious, happy place to live that's designed to suit their unique needs. Elephants need a lot of room to roam and ponds to swim in. Birds need space to fly and plenty of perches. And pigs need barns with soft hay for sleeping. Sanctuaries offer animals these spaces—and employ a lot of workers to maintain them and to keep the animals fed and healthy.

Would you like to work at a sanctuary and spend time with your favourite animals?

Be a Super-Scientist

Scientists and inventors can come up with amazing new products that help humans and animals. For example, scientists created the SynFrog model frog that you read about earlier. Students are dissecting them instead of real frogs. Scientists also developed "organs-on-a-chip", which are tiny devices that function just like human organs. Because of this, many tests that used to be done on animals are now done on chips!

Can you think of an invention that would save animals' lives?

Robots Are for More Than Playing

If you think robots are awesome, why not design

one that helps animals? Delle is a robotic dolphin that people may one day swim with at marine parks. When people choose to have a blast with robotic dolphins, real dolphins won't be taken from their homes in the sea and confined to concrete tanks.

What type of robot would you design?

Write Your Heart Out

If you like storytelling, why not write a book like *Charlotte's Web*, *Black Beauty*, or even the one you're reading right now? Many children's books have important messages that teach kids to be kind to animals.

Or you could be a reporter and share news involving animals. Maybe you could report on how someone saved a dog from a locked, hot car, how a community saved a forest that's home to many animals, or how a new law will protect endangered species.

Do you love to write?

Teach Kindness

You could become an educator and help create a kinder world by teaching young people to respect animals. You could assign fun activities like having your students research their favourite animals and present their findings to the class. Or you could ask them to participate in a project to benefit the local animal shelter.

Do you dream of teaching others about animals and how to help them?

Work for an Animal Organization

Animal organizations, like PETA India, exist for a good cause. They need employees to help raise money, create their website and plan exciting events like vegan food giveaways and educational street-theatre style plays. Some workers create videos to help animals get adopted, some have meetings with companies and show them how to be kinder, and others keep the ambulances used to transport animals running smoothly. Animal organizations need people to do almost every job you can think of!

What other kinds of workers would an animal organization need?

Cook Up Kindness

These days, many good cooks are making tasty vegan meals—ones without animal flesh, eggs or milk. If you love cooking, you could make vegan food for a restaurant, food truck or bakery—or even open one of your own. Vegan restaurants are popping up all over! Or you could be a food scientist and research and test new foods. Food scientists invent yummy vegan foods like the GoodDot keema, which is made without meat!

Do you see yourself designing the menu for your very own vegan restaurant someday?

Make a Fashion Statement

Do you like shopping for clothes or even thinking up designs of your own? Caring fashion designers are creating stylish clothes, shoes and bags using materials that didn't come from animals. Did you know that vegan leather can be made from pineapples, apples, mushrooms and other animal-friendly materials? There are humane alternatives to sheep's wool, animal fur and duck and goose feathers, too. As a fashion designer, you could help people dress compassionately by creating cruelty-free outfits that everyone would want to wear!

What are some other materials that don't come from animals that could be used for clothing?

Be Artsy for Animals

Can you paint or draw? Why not use those talents to benefit animals? Maybe you could be a graphic designer who creates designs by hand or by using computer software to make posters and other artwork for an organization that helps animals.

You could even make sculptures. One artist created an exhibit for PETA called The Council of Animals (What to Do About the Humans). He made big metal statues of a polar bear, a chicken, a coyote, an elephant and a rhinoceros. The sculptures were displayed in Washington, D.C.! Lots of visitors came to see the animals, and the coyote (with the help of an actor's voice) explained to them how they could be kind.

Do you think creating art to help animals is in your future?

*****

No matter what you're good at or what you love to do, there's almost always a way you can use your talents and interests to create a better world for animals. And the best part is that you don't even have to wait until you're older. Turn to the next chapter to see how you can make many animals' lives better right now!

How to Be a Hero for Animals

You can help animals every day. Whether it's your dog or cat at home, the birds in your backyard, the whales in the deepest oceans, the tigers in circuses, or the rabbits in laboratories, you can help make the world a better place for them. Are you ready to find out how you can be a hero for animals?

Help Animals From Home

- When an insect accidentally winds up inside your home, you can carefully move them back outside. Gently cover them with a cup and then carefully slide a thin piece of cardboard or paper beneath the cup. Then carry the insect outside or to the nearest window. When you're outside or at a window, take away the cardboard or paper and let the insect go.

- Put a shallow dish of water outside for thirsty birds and other animals, especially on hot days.

Be sure to keep it clean (free of dirt and algae), and put a stick in it so that insects who fall in don't drown.

- Ask an adult in your home to buy cruelty-free soap, toothpaste, household cleaners, and other products. Remember reading about how some humans perform cruel experiments on animals? Well, products that are cruelty-free aren't tested on animals. Look for labels that say "Cruelty-Free" or "Not Tested on Animals". Or visit **https://crueltyfree.peta.org/** to see a list of brands to look for.

- Invite your friends over for a movie night! Watch an animal-friendly movie like *Babe*, *Chicken Run: Dawn of the Nugget*, *Finding Dory*, *Horton Hears a Who*, *The One and Only Ivan*, or *The Secret Life of Pets*.

- Make vegan food for your family and friends to show them that it's easy to eat yummy meals without using meat, eggs, or dairy, which come from animals. For fun and easy recipes to try, go to **PETAKids.com/Recipes**.

- When you need new shoes or clothes, choose items that were made without taking anything from animals. Foxes, sheep, cows, geese and other animals need their fur, wool, skin or feathers, just as we need our skin and hair. When you shop for shoes and clothes, just check the tags. Stay away from ones that say “fur”, “wool”, “leather”, and “down”, and choose the ones that say “faux fur”, “man-made materials”, “synthetic”, “cotton”, “polyester”, “rayon”, or “viscose”.

- Ask your family, friends, and neighbours to have their dogs and cats spayed or neutered (sterilized). There are already too many animals waiting for good homes, and spaying or neutering prevents cats and dogs from having babies. It’s also healthy for them.

- When you’re walking your dog, let them stop and sniff interesting scents. Dogs can detect many more smells than we can, and they learn a lot through their noses. Knowing all the neighbourhood aromas can help if they get lost. Make sure your dog gets playtime too, and let them be silly! You can also give old blankets, towels, and dog or cat toys to a local animal shelter.

- Plant sunflowers and other plants that provide food for birds, butterflies, bees, and other pollinators. You could even add a birdhouse, birdfeeder, or birdbath.

- Create art on posters, paint on t-shirts or use chalk on sidewalks with animal-friendly messages like “Be Nice to All Animals”, “Animals Are Friends, Not Food”, “Milk Is for Baby Cows”, “Animals Are Someone, Not Something”, or “Adopt—Don’t Shop”.

Be a Superhero for Animals While You're at School

- If your class plans to dissect frogs, worms, or other animals, just say no. Ask your teacher for an assignment that doesn't hurt animals. You might be surprised with how many other students join you! And if you need help, contact PETA India.

- Start an animal rights club to meet other kids who also want to help animals. Invite friends and classmates to join your club, and ask teachers to sponsor it.

- If your mother packs your tiffin box for school, request her to pack it with delicious vegan items. Did you know most of the food you eat is already vegan like apples, subzi, daal and cucumber and tomato sandwiches? When it comes to food, vegan simply means made from plants.

- If your teacher lets you choose a topic to research and write about or give a presentation on, pick a topic about animals that you want to learn more about, like animal testing or vegan food.

- If your school is planning a field trip to a zoo, speak up. Start a petition asking to go to a kind location, like an animal-free circus, a botanical garden, a space center, a science museum, an amusement park or a water park—or to take a trip to see animals living in their natural environment. Kind places that take care of animals and allow them to live in peaceful, spacious, natural habitats with members of their own species—not in small cages. They don't make them give rides or be held by strangers for selfies, which is frightening for the animals. Circuses, aquariums and marine mammal parks keep animals in unnatural enclosures and often make them do confusing tricks. Consider running for student council to help make sure your school plans animal-friendly trips in the future.

- Make sure your school doesn't use cruel mouse traps, and talk to your principal about why live traps are the compassionate choice.

- Cover your textbooks and notebooks with homemade book covers and decorate them with "kindness to animals" messages.

- If your teacher plans to get a "classroom pet", explain why animals shouldn't be kept in classrooms. Sometimes animals get handled roughly and even get injured by students who don't know how to care for them, or are left alone for long periods of time when school is out. A better idea is for your class to "adopt" an animal at a sanctuary. You can ask to receive photos of the animal and updates on how they're doing. And your class can raise money for their food and care. Many sanctuaries offer virtual visits with your adopted animal. And if you live close enough, you can even plan a trip to visit them in person! Ask your teacher to get information about these sanctuaries from **TeachKind.org**. If there's already an animal in your classroom, remind others to treat them with kindness and respect.

Take Action While Out and About

- If you see someone being mean to an animal, politely ask them to stop—and tell an adult right away.

- Don't chase birds. It scares them and can make them leave their nest or babies unattended.

- Wear shirts and buttons with animal rights messages. Check out the cool shirts at **https://styched.life/collections/peta**. Or make your own at home—all you need is a blank shirt and fabric markers or paint.

- Littering hurts animals, so always put your trash in a garbage can and your bottles, cans, and other recyclable materials in the correct bins.

- Clean up ponds, rivers, beaches, and other habitats for the fish, turtles, frogs, birds and other cool animals who live there by going "trash fishing"! "Catching" trash (instead of fish) is a fun way to spend time with your family and friends outdoors.

And unlike regular fishing, it doesn't hurt smart, interesting fish or other animals.

- When you're observing animals in the wild, be sure to keep a respectful distance and never touch or harass them.

- Donkeys, camels, horses, elephants, dolphins and other animals don't want to be used for rides. Instead, ride a trolley, a go-kart, an air boat or a paddle boat, or go zip-lining, parasailing or snorkeling. There are endless ways to have fun while being kind to animals.

Glossary

animal sanctuary: a safe place where animals can live after they've been rescued from abusive places like circuses or laboratories (A true sanctuary puts the needs and wants of animals first. Some places that confine animals to small enclosures or let people handle wild animals for photos call themselves "sanctuaries" or "rescues", but they do this just to bring in paying customers.)

burrows: holes or tunnels in the ground that animals make for shelter or protection

compass: a tool used to determine directions that has a magnetic needle that always points north

crop milk: a milky liquid that adult pigeons and certain other birds produce in their crop (part of the digestive system) to feed their young

dissect: traditionally, the act of cutting up and studying once-living beings (Students today are increasingly choosing non-animal methods of dissection.)

empathy: imagining how someone else is feeling by putting yourself in their place

fungus: living things, such as molds and mushrooms, that usually grow on plants or on dead or decaying matter

GoFundMe: an online fundraising platform that allows individuals to collect donations to support a project or cause

great apes: any of several large primates, including the orangutan, gorilla, chimpanzee, and bonobo (Did you know humans are great apes? Even though we might do some things differently from other animals, we're animals, too. We all share the planet, and it's important to be kind to everyone!)

groom: to clean oneself or another animal, such as by brushing or licking (For example, a mouse may lick another mouse's fur or a human's finger, as mentioned in Chapter 2.)

humane live trap: a special kind of trap that helps catch animals, like mice, without hurting them (When a mouse goes inside the trap, a door closes behind them. Then you can take the trap outside and release the animal back into their natural home. It's important to be kind to all animals, even the ones we don't want in our houses.)

idioms: expressions that do not literally mean what they say (For example, if you call something a "piece of cake", it doesn't refer to an actual cake. It means that you think something is really easy to do. Some idioms are harmful because they refer to violence toward animals, like "kill two birds with one stone", which means to accomplish two things with only one action. It's nicer to say, "feed two birds with one scone".)

loom: a frame or machine used to weave thread or yarn into cloth

magnetic field: an invisible area surrounding magnets or electric currents where magnetic forces can be detected

matriarch: a female who leads her family or social group

migration: a journey from one part of the world to another for food, better weather, or a safer place to live (Animals who migrate often move back and forth from summer to winter homes.)

organs-on-a-chip: like tiny laboratories, as small as a computer chip, that scientists use to study how human organs work (Imagine if you could make a mini version of your heart or lungs on a tiny computer chip. That's what these chips do. They use human cells to create a model of an organ. This lets scientists see how the organ reacts to different medicines or diseases, without having to test on animals.)

pain receptors: nerve endings in your body that can sense pain

short: when the flow of electricity in a circuit travels in the wrong direction, often causing lights or electrical devices to shut off

speciesism: the belief that one kind of animal is more important than another kind or that some species deserve to be treated with kindness, while others don't (Everyone deserves to be treated with respect and kindness, whether they're a human, a dog, a pig, or any other species.)

SynFrog: a super-realistic fake frog that's replacing real frogs in classroom dissection activities (You can cut open SynFrog, which even has guts and organs, to take a look inside without hurting animals!)

talons: a bird's long, sharp claws

vegan: someone who doesn't eat any foods that come from animals, such as meat, eggs, and dairy; food that doesn't have any ingredients that came from animals

About the Author

Ingrid Newkirk spent her childhood in New Delhi, Kodai Kanal, and Shimla. She is the founder of PETA India and all PETA affiliates internationally. Since 1980, she has inspired countless people to live by this simple rule: Never be silent if an animal is suffering, and never steal from, harm, or kill any living being.

About the Illustrator

Samantha Skeels of Heroic Art & Design lives in New Hampshire, USA and is an illustrator, graphic artist and musician.

HarperCollins *Publishers* India

At HarperCollins India, we believe in telling the best stories and finding the widest readership for our books in every format possible. We started publishing in 1992; a great deal has changed since then, but what has remained constant is the passion with which our authors write their books, the love with which readers receive them, and the sheer joy and excitement that we as publishers feel in being a part of the publishing process.

Over the years, we've had the pleasure of publishing some of the finest writing from the subcontinent and around the world, including several award-winning titles and some of the biggest bestsellers in India's publishing history. But nothing has meant more to us than the fact that millions of people have read the books we published, and that somewhere, a book of ours might have made a difference.

As we look to the future, we go back to that one word—a word which has been a driving force for us all these years.

Read.